J

353.03 Beckman, Beatrice
BE
 I can be a
 president

$13.27

I CAN BE

PRESIDENT

By Beatrice Beckman

Prepared under the direction of Robert Hillerich, Ph.D.

CHILDRENS PRESS ™

CHICAGO

Library of Congress Cataloging in Publication Data

Beckman, Beatrice.
  I can be President

  Summary: Describes in simple terms the duties
and responsibilities of the President of the United
States.
  1. Presidents—United States—Juvenile literature.
[1. Presidents] I. Title. II. Title: President
JK517.B43 1984   353.031   84-12653
ISBN 0-516-01841-8

PICTURE DICTIONARY

lawmakers

congress

armed forces

commander
in
chief

groups

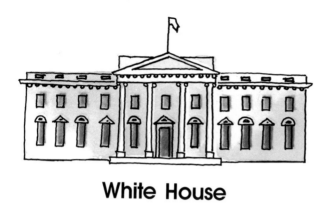

White House

Oval Office

president's cabinet

Constitution

political parties

college

head of state

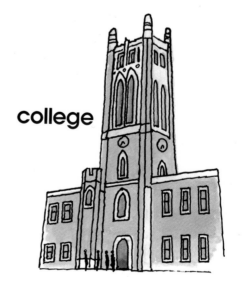

President Dwight D. Eisenhower, the thirty-fourth president
of the United States, served from 1953 to 1961. In 1953 he
threw out the first ball of the baseball season.

It is the start of the baseball season. The stands are filled. The game is about to begin.

The president of the United States stands. He throws out the first ball.

President Ronald Reagan talks to the lawmakers in Congress.

Another day, both houses of Congress are waiting. They are the lawmakers. The president of the United States enters. He walks to the front of the room.

The president tells Congress how the country is doing. He talks about new laws the country needs.

These are two very different jobs. The president is responsible for both. The first one is part of his work as head of state. The head of state of any country stands for all the people of that country.

head of state

Top: Standing in front of the space shuttle, *Enterprise*, President Reagan waves to the people who came to see him.

Left: President Gerald Ford, who served as president from 1974 to 1977, talks to Leonid Brezhnev, leader of the Union of Soviet Socialist Republics (Russia).

Above: President Jimmy Carter welcomes Prince Faud of Saudi Arabia. Carter was president from 1977 to 1981.

The president does many things in the name of the American people. He welcomes important people from other countries. He gives speeches. He lights the big Christmas tree outside the White House. The president does these things and more.

President Gerald Ford (top) and
President Jimmy Carter (bottom) sign laws.

Part of the president's job is to see that the country works well. He also sees that its laws are carried out.

He reads the laws that Congress wants to pass. If the president thinks the laws are good, he signs them. If not, he may send them back to Congress for changes.

North entrance to the White House (left) and south side of the
White House (right). President Reagan (below) signs the
law that made Martin Luther King's birthday a national holiday.

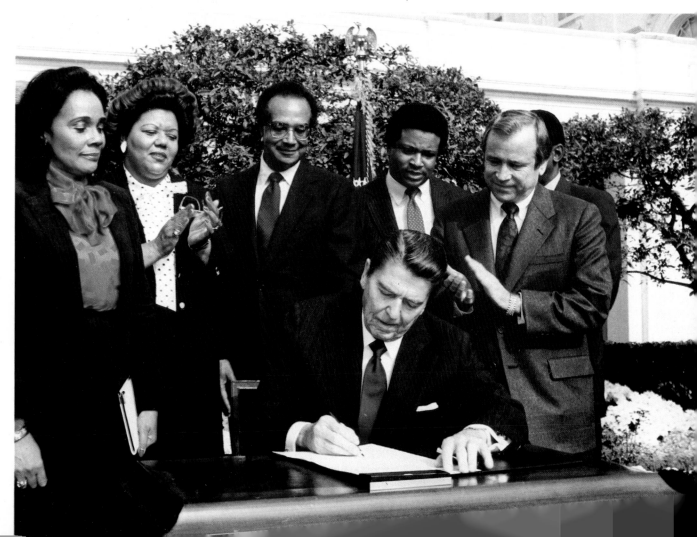

The president lives in the White House in Washington, D.C. He works in a beautiful office. It is called the Oval Office. He spends long hours working there.

White House

Oval Office

In one day, the president meets with many people. Some meetings are about things in our country. Others are about other countries.

President Anwar el-Sadat of Egypt (left), President Jimmy Carter (center), and Prime Minister Menachem Begin of Israel (right) sign a treaty that ended the state of war between Israel and Egypt.

President John F. Kennedy talks with Jawaharlal Nehru, prime minister of India, in the Oval Office of the White House.

President Reagan welcomes a young soccer team (left)
and awards a hero's medal to a soldier (right).

Each day the president
usually has visits from
special people. Some
may be from other
countries. Some may be
Americans. One
American may have won
a contest. Another may
be a hero.

President Gerald Ford talks with Secretary of State Henry Kissinger.

president's cabinet

A president's job is too much work for one person. So the president has people help him. Some of these people are called the president's cabinet.

The idea of a cabinet came from George

George Washington
was president of
the United States
from 1789 to 1797.

Washington. He was the
first president of the
United States. Washington
asked four men to help
him. Together they would
decide what was best for
the new country.

President Washington's first cabinet, from left to right,
General Henry Knox (secretary of war),
Alexander Hamilton (secretary of the treasury),
Thomas Jefferson (secretary of state), and
Edmond Randolph (attorney general)

Thomas Jefferson helped George Washington. He was secretary of state. Jefferson later became the third president of the United States.

Other people help the president do his job. George Washington had two people. One was his nephew. The other had been with Washington during the Revolution. Washington paid both men himself.

Presidents are always busy. Many people
help them do their job.

Today about eighty people help the president. Some write speeches. Several deal with the news. Some handle the mail. The rest work at other jobs.

The president is also commander in chief of the armed forces. He is head of those forces in peace and war.

armed forces

commander
in chief

The president decides who will hold the highest jobs in the armed forces. He sees that the armed forces have enough people in times of peace. He also sees that they are used wisely in times of war.

The president decides how we deal with other countries. He must know what is happening in the world. And he must decide the best way to

Left: African leaders visit President John F. Kennedy in the Oval Office of the White House.
Right: President Ford flew to Japan to talk to that country's leaders.

get along with the rest of the world.

The president has one more job. He is the leader of his political party. He stands for what his party believes.

John F. Kennedy was forty-three when he was elected president. His son John was just a baby when he was in office.

Ronald Reagan was sixty-nine when he was elected president.

So far, all the presidents
of the United States have
been men. But one day
a woman may be

Constitution

president. The
Constitution gives only
three rules for becoming
president. Presidents must
be born in the United
States. They must be at
least thirty-five years old.
And they must have lived
in the United States for
fourteen years.

President Ford visited Poland.

President Carter talked to farmers in California.

But people who want
to be president must be
even more. They must be
leaders. They must know
and care about this
country. They must know
and care about other
countries.

groups

college

Would you like to be president of the United States? If so, you must start working now. Take part in school groups. Work with neighborhood groups. Join other groups. Become a leader.

You will have to study hard. Plan to go to college. Keep up with the news. Know what is going on in the world. Even so,

The presidential seal is on the stand in front of President Carter. At important ceremonies the band plays "Hail to the Chief," the official song of the president of the United States, when the president enters.

you can't be sure you will become president. But just maybe one day a band will play "Hail to the Chief" when you enter a room.

WORDS YOU SHOULD KNOW

baseball (BAYSS • bawl)—a game played by two teams of nine people each on a field that has four bases.

cabinet (KAB • ih • nit)—a group of people who help the president decide what is best for the country. Each person heads a different office.

college (KAHL • ij)—a school for higher learning that follows high school.

commander in chief (kuh • MAN • der in cheef)—the person who has the final say about everything the armed forces do

Congress (KAHNG • griss)—the body that makes the laws of the United States. It has two houses, called the Senate and the House of Representatives.

constitution (kahn • stih • TOO • shun)—a paper that lists the rules that everyone must follow. Countries, states, and clubs may have constitutions.

deal (DEEL)—to have to do with

forces (FORSS • iz)—all the people in the army, navy, and other branches that protect the country

hail (HAYL)—a word used to show that people are glad and proud to see someone

hero (HEER • oh)—a person who has done a brave act

law (LAW)—a rule that all the people must follow

lawmakers (LAW • may • kerz)—the people who make the laws

leader (LEED • er)—a person who shows others how to do things or who goes ahead to show the way

nephew (NEF • yoo)—the son of someone's brother or sister

office (AW • fiss)—the room in which someone works or a special job that someone holds

peace (PEECE)—a time when there is no war

political (puh • LIT • ih • kil)—having to do with the way a country is run or the way a party believes it should be run

president (PREZ • ih • dent)—the highest office in the United States. It also means the chief of a company, a college, or a club.

responsible (ri • SPAHN • sih • bil)—having to answer for doing something as part of one's job

season (SEE • zun)—one of the four times of year called spring, summer, fall, and winter

secretary of state (SEK • ruh • tare • ee uv STAYT)—the person who heads the office that deals with the United States and its place in the world

speech (SPEECH)—a talk that is given to a group of people

staff (STAF)—a group of people who work to help a leader

state (STAYT)—a country. In the United States, it also means one of the fifty parts of the country.

study (STUHD • ee)—to try to learn by reading and thinking

welcome (WEL • kum)—to give people the feeling that their visit makes everyone happy

INDEX

age of president, 25
armed forces, 22
baseball, first ball 5
cabinet, 16, 17
college, 28
commander in chief
  of the armed forces, 22
Congress, 6, 11
Constitution, 25
countries, other, 9, 13, 23, 27
first president of the United States, 17
groups, 28
"Hail to the Chief," 29
head of state, 7
Jefferson, Thomas, 18
lawmakers, 6
laws, 7, 11

leaders, 27, 28
mail, 21
meets new people, 21
other countries, 9, 13, 23
oval office, 13
peace, 22
political party, 23
rules for becoming president, 25
school, 28
secretary of state, 18
signs laws, 11
speeches, 9, 21
staff, 19, 21
third president of the United States, 18
visits with president, 15
war, 22
Washington, D.C., 13
Washington, George, 17, 19
White House, 13

PHOTO CREDITS
©Mark Kauffman/Sports Illustrated—4
THE WHITE HOUSE/Official Photograph:
  Bill Fitz-Patrick—6, 8 (top), 15 (left);
  Pete Souza—12 (bottom);
  Karl Schumacher—15 (right);
  Dave Valdez—24 (bottom);
  Michael Evans—29 (right);
BLACK STAR:
  © Dennis Brack—8 (bottom left & right), 10 (2 photos),
                  16, 20 (3 photos), 26 (2 photos);
  © Owen D. B.—14 (top);
  © Eiji Miyazawa—23 (right);
  © Bart Photo—29 (left)

Washington, D.C. Convention and Visitors Association—
12 (top, 2 photos)

John F. Kennedy Library—14 (bottom), 23 (left), 24 (top)

Historical Pictures Services, Chicago—17, 18

Journalism Service, Inc.:
  © Joseph Jacobson—Cover

ABOUT THE AUTHOR

Beatrice Beckman is a former teacher of English. She later turned to educational publishing where she was the editorial director of language arts and early childhood programs. A native New Yorker, Ms. Beckman lives in Chicago where she works as a free-lance writer and editor. *I Can Be President* is her first book for Childrens Press.